# Land of the Bible

# Land of the Bible

by
Paul S. Newman

Photographs by
Adrian Williams

The C.R. Gibson Company, *Publishers*, Norwalk, Connecticut

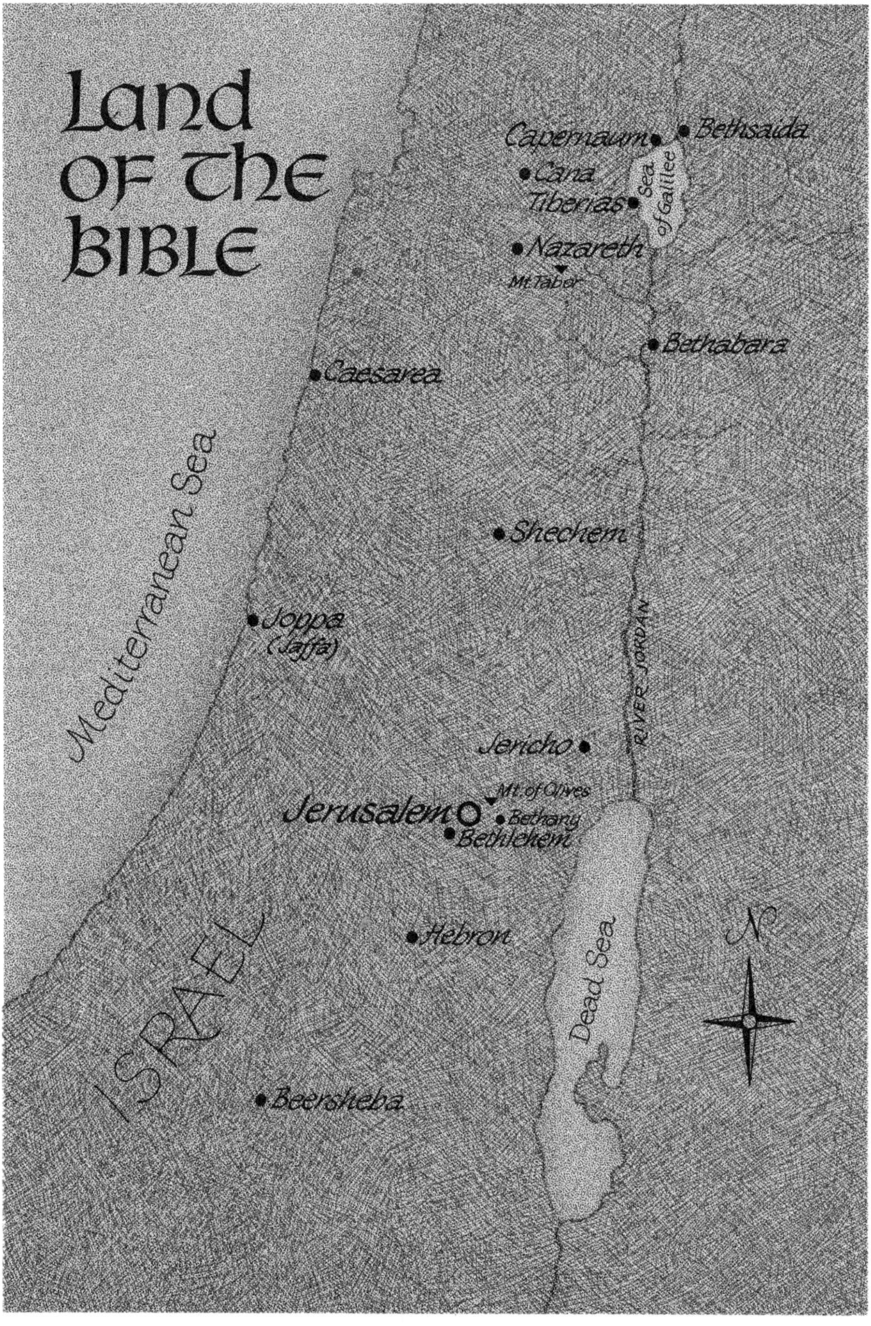

Land
of the
Bible

Bethsaida

Capernaum
Cana
Tiberias
Sea of Galilee

Nazareth
Mt Tabor

Bethabara

Caesarea

Mediterranean Sea

Shechem

RIVER JORDAN

Joppa
(Jaffa)

Jericho

Jerusalem
Mt of Olives
Bethany
Bethlehem

Hebron

Dead Sea

N

ISRAEL

Beersheba

# CONTENTS

**Jerusalem** – *The Golden Gate through which it is said Jesus entered Jerusalem.*

# JERUSALEM

*"If I forget thee, O Jerusalem, let my right hand forget her cunning."* PSALM 137:5.

Crowning a rocky plateau that rises some 2,500 feet, Jerusalem is bounded on the south and west by the Valley of Hinnom, on the east by the Kidron Valley and is open toward the north. Until 1858, Jerusalem was totally contained inside its 16th century walls. Today, it pushes beyond those walls.

Originally, it was a Jebusite town, whose inhabitants boasted that it was so well fortified that it could be defended by the "blind and the lame". David entered the city through a tunnel or water shaft that led to a spring. He called it the City of David. To avert a plague, the prophet Gad told David that he must make an offering on a nearby hill. He probably used the great rock that now lies under the Dome of the Rock for his altar. This also marks the likely site of Solomon's great temple.

While David brought the Ark of the Covenant to Jerusalem, it was Solomon who housed it inside his magnificent temple.

When Jesus visited Jerusalem, the temple He entered was a recently restored one. Under Herod, much of Jerusalem had been rebuilt. He refortified the city, set up the Antonia fortress to guard the Temple Enclosure, erected his own palace with its triple towers, as well as offended the Jewish citizens by building a theater and gymnasium.

In over 3,000 years, Jerusalem has suffered through more than twenty sieges, been despoiled by Nebuchadnezzar and Hadrian, and changed from one religion to another six times.

But to Jews, scattered in exile throughout the world, returning to pray at the wall of Solomon's Temple has always been a fervent goal. To the Crusader, rescuing the site of Jesus' crucifixion from the infidel prompted his perilous pilgrimage during the Middle Ages. To the Moslem, this is the third holiest city. And the hope of all mankind lies in the translation of its earliest name "Urusalim"—foundation, or city of peace.

**Tower of David** – *Part of the Citadel built by Herod the Great in Jerusalem.*

# THE TOWER OF DAVID

*"So David dwelt in the fort, and called it the city of David. And David built round about from Millo and inward."*

About 1,000 B.C., David captured the walled city of the Jebusites, where Jerusalem now lies and made it his capital. He fortified it and brought the Ark of the Covenant within its walls. Since David's time, Jerusalem has been partially or completely destroyed some eighteen times.

When Herod the Great built his great palace just before the time of Jesus, he raised three stone towers to protect it on the northern side. The towers were called Phasael for his brother, Hippicus, a friend, and Mariamne, his wife. Of these only the foundations of the tallest tower are still standing today and it is known as the Tower of David. Herod built on the ruins of an old fortification and recent excavation at the Tower suggests that these ruins may date back to David's time.

The present Tower of David is about sixty feet high, but on top of the original tower, Herod had built luxurious apartments which almost doubled the tower's height.

The three towers of Herod protected a corner of his palace and guarded the nearby Jaffa Gate. When Titus captured and destroyed Jerusalem in A.D. 70, he left the three towers standing to show all viewers a sample of the mighty walls that his legions had overcome.

The ruins of Herod's palace were built upon and used by other conquerors, the Crusaders, the Mamelukes and the Turks. The present structure, called the Citadel, and its outer walls and tower are mostly fourteenth century Mameluke work. The Crusaders gave the Citadel its currently popular name, the Tower of David. Today the Tower of David is used as the dramatic setting for a sound and light show.

**Dead Sea Scrolls** — *Ancient writings typical of those found in the Shrine of the Book.*

# SHRINE OF THE BOOK

*"Hear, O heavens, and give ear, O earth: for the LORD hath spoken, I have nourished and brought up children, and they have rebelled against me."* ISAIAH 1:2.

The earliest known Hebrew manuscript of the text of Isaiah may be seen inside the dramatically contemporary Shrine of the Book.

In 1947, a Bedouin youth searching for a missing goat near the Dead Sea, entered a cave of the Khirbet Qumran region. Inside, he found several ancient jars and hidden in the jars were seven scrolls. They dated from shortly before the time of Jesus up to the end of the Second Jewish Revolt, in A.D. 135.

The scrolls consist of both Biblical passages and sectarian writing. The sect that lived in this arid wasteland was probably the Essenes, an ascetic group, who believed in the coming "End of Days", and as "Sons of Light" sought to separate themselves from the rest of mankind.

The most important of the seven scrolls is a complete Hebrew version of the Book of the Prophet Isaiah, which is about 1,000 years earlier than any previously known Hebrew text of this Book. When unrolled, this ancient parchment scroll is over twenty feet long.

Among the sectarian scrolls is the "Rule of the Community", dealing with details of every day life. It describes how one should eat at the communal meals, the initiation and the oath required of anyone joining the select community.

The Shrine of the Book contains other scrolls, letters and articles such as mirrors, jugs and even a key from the time when Christianity had its origin.

**Dome of the Rock** – *A holy place to Christians, Jews and Muslims, and the site of Abraham's sacrifice.*

# DOME OF THE ROCK

*"And he said, Take now thy son, thine only son Isaac, whom thou lovest, and get thee into the land of Moriah; and offer him there for a burnt offering upon one of the mountains . . . "*GENESIS 22:2.

Traditionally, Mount Moriah in Jerusalem has been considered the place where at the last moment God kept Abraham from sacrificing Isaac. On the hill is a large rock, which may have served as the sacrificial altar.

When the prophet Gad advised David to make an offering to spare Jerusalem from the plague, David used the same great rock for his altar. Measuring fifty-eight feet in length and fifty-one feet in width, it probably served as the altar of Solomon's Temple, which was erected here shortly around the middle of the ninth century before Christ. The rock is the traditional site of the prophet Mohammed's ascent into heaven.

Solomon's Temple was burned by the Babylonians about 586 B.C. and rebuilt by Zerubbabel around 515 B.C. But the Holy of Holies, the sacred inner sanctuary, no longer contained the Ark of the Covenant.

About 20 B.C., Herod the Great constructed a larger, more striking Temple on this site. It was from the courtyard of Herod's Temple that Jesus drove out the moneychangers.

In A.D. 70, on the anniversary of the burning of Solomon's Temple, the Romans burned down Herod's magnificent Temple. For a time, a Temple of Jupiter was raised here and Jews were allowed into Jerusalem only on special holidays.

When the Moslems conquered Jerusalem in the seventh century, they raised the Dome of the Rock over the ancient site to commemorate Mohammed's ascent unto heaven. In 1099, the Crusaders captured the shrine and converted it into a church. But in 1187, Saladin recaptured it and the Dome of the Rock became a Moslem shrine again.

**Mount of Olives** — *The Mount of Olives showing the Church of All Nations in the foreground.*

# MOUNT OF OLIVES

*"And when he was come nigh, even now at the descent of the mount of Olives, the whole multitude of the disciples began to rejoice and praise God with a loud voice for all the mighty works that they had seen; Saying, Blessed be the King that cometh in the name of the Lord: peace in heaven, and glory in the highest."* LUKE: 19:37-38.

As Jesus was descending the Mount of Olives, the multitude welcomed Him. When He came over the crest and saw Jerusalem looming before Him, Jesus wept, predicting its destruction and the leveling of Herod's Temple. The Ascension of Jesus took place before the eyes of the Apostles on the Mount of Olives.

Long a holy site, the Mount of Olives was where a barefoot David fled when Absalom, his son, challenged his rule. Ezekiel beheld a vision of God's glory here.

The Emperor Constantine built a basilica over the spot where Jesus was believed to have ascended. When the Persians destroyed the church and others in and around Jerusalem, this was one of the few to be quickly rebuilt. A seventh century pilgrim states that inside one could see the last footprints of Jesus before He ascended into heaven. The Crusaders repaired the church, but the present Chapel of Ascension got its mosque-style dome when Saladin conquered Jerusalem in 1187.

Nearby on the slope is the Franciscan Chapel of Dominus Flavit, marking the place where Jesus wept.

At the base of the Mount are Biblical tombs including those of Absalom, Zachariah and St. James. The area contains an ancient Jewish cemetery. Believing that the Messiah would enter Jerusalem from this direction, many sought to be buried here, expecting that would make them the first to be resurrected.

**The Upper Room** – *The place of the Last Supper, located on Mount Zion in Jerusalem.*

# MOUNT ZION

*"Now the first day of the feast of the unleavened bread the disciples came to Jesus, saying unto him, Where wilt thou that we prepare for thee to eat the passover?* MATTHEW 26:17.

When Jesus went with the twelve disciples into Jerusalem for the passover meal, He predicted that one among them would betray him. The house where the Lord's Supper was held is believed to have been on Mount Zion.

Located partly outside the walls of present day Jerusalem, Mount Zion is the site of several important religious shrines. Built by Crusaders the mosque-like building here houses both the Tomb of David and the Coenaculum, or room of the Last Supper.

On the building's lower level is a chamber containing the large stone coffin in which David is supposed to lie. The top floor has been restored in the Gothic style of the Crusaders and here Jesus and His disciples feasted in an "upper room" (Luke 22:12). The Pentecostal Miracle, when the Holy Spirit appeared, also occured in this room.

Mount Zion, one of Jerusalem's southern hills, is where David established his capital. When David brought the long missing sacred Ark of the Covenant to Jerusalem, it was kept at Mount Zion till Solomon had it placed in the Holy of Holies in his Temple on Mount Moriah. The Ark was a chest slightly longer than a yard lined inside with gold and covered by a solid gold lid. It contained tables of stone upon which was written the testimony of God to the Children of Israel.

Nearby on the hill is the modern Abbey of the Dormition, where tradition states that Mary fell into her eternal sleep.

**Garden of Gethsemane** — *The path leading to the Garden of Gethsemane where Jesus prayed.*

# GETHSEMANE

*"Then cometh Jesus with them unto a place called Geth-semane, and saith unto the disciples, Sit ye here, while I go and pray yonder."* MATTHEW 26:36.

Jesus often enjoyed the tranquility of the garden of Geth-semane at the foot of the Mount of Olives. It was to this quiet place that Jesus came with Peter, James, and John to pray and it is the scene of His agony. Here Judas Iscariot betrayed Jesus with a kiss thus identifying Him to the armed men who arrested Him.

The name Gethsemane means "oil press" and the slope of the Mount is still covered with olive trees on the Mount. While many of the present olive trees are well over a thousand years old, they probably do not date back to the days of Jesus. In A.D. 70, when Titus beseiged Jerusalem, he had all the trees around the city cut down.

In 1848, the Franciscans enclosed the garden with a stone wall. When they erected the Church of All Nations here in 1919, they found the ruins of two previous churches beneath it. One was from the fourth century and had been destroyed by the Persians in 614. On its ruins the Crusaders had built the second church in the twelfth century. Just as the previous builders had done, the Franciscans avoided covering the nearby great rock, which may have been the Rock of Agony, where Jesus prayed.

Within walking distance from the lovely walled garden is the Tomb of the Virgin Mary. As far back as the sixth century, Mary is said to have been buried here. The present Abbey of St. Mary was built in the twelfth century by the Crusaders and inside, marble steps lead to the underground site of the tomb of Jesus' mother.

On the slope above is the onion-domed Russian Church of Mary Magdalene. Built in 1888 by Czar Alexander of Russia, the church contains the preserved hearts of some members of the royal Romanov family. This church claims that it marks the site of Gethsemane.

**Via Dolorosa —** *In the background the Ecce Homo Arch, where Pilate presented Jesus to the crowd.*

# VIA DOLOROSA

*"Then came Jesus forth, wearing the crown of thorns, and the purple robe. And Pilate saith unto them, Behold the man!"*
JOHN 19:5.

The Via Dolorosa is the route taken by Jesus from the place of His trial to His Crucifixion. Called the Way of the Cross, there are fourteen stations along the Via Dolorosa marking the events in the Gospels.

The trial of Jesus was held in the Antonia, a fortress at the northern corner of the Temple Enclosure, built on the site of an earlier stronghold. Herod the Great repaired and fortified it to protect his new Temple. It was into the Antonia that Paul fled from the mob at the Temple. Today, its site is marked by the Convent of Our Lady of Zion which is the first station.

At the second station, Jesus received the Cross.

The third, marked today by the Ecce Homo Arch, is where Pilate presented Jesus to the crowd.

At the fourth station, Jesus met Mary, His mother.

At the fifth station, Simon the Cyrene helped Jesus carry the Cross.

At the sixth station, Veronica wiped Jesus' face.

At the seventh, Jesus fell. The Judicial Gate.

At the eight, Jesus spoke to the women of Jerusalem.

At the ninth, Jesus fell again.

The last five stations are all located within the Compound of the Holy Sepulchre.

At the tenth station, Jesus' garments were stripped from Him.

At the eleventh, Jesus was nailed to the Cross.

At the twelfth, Jesus died on the Cross.

At the thirteenth, Jesus was taken from the Cross.

At the fourteenth, Jesus was placed in the Holy Sepulchre.

Every Friday at 3 P.M., a pilgrims' procession follows the route of the fourteen Stations of the Cross.

**Holy Sepulchre** — *Church of the Holy Sepulchre built where Jesus is believed to have been buried.*

# HOLY SEPULCHRE

*"And when Joseph had taken the body, he wrapped it in a clean linen cloth, And laid it in his own new tomb, which he had hewn out in the rock: and he rolled a great stone to the door of the sepulchre, and departed."* MATTHEW 27:59-60.

The Holy Sepulchre where Jesus was buried is the fourteenth and final Station of the Cross. It is inside the Church of the Holy Sepulchre.

The tomb belonged to Joseph of Arimathaea. He was a Jew who believed in Jesus, and although he was a member of the Sanhedrin or ruling council, he had not agreed to Jesus being put to death.

It was in this tomb that Jesus remained from sundown on Friday until sunrise Sunday.

After Titus destroyed Jerusalem in A.D. 70, a shrine to Venus was placed over the site of the tomb. About 326, the Emperor Constantine the Great ordered the shrine removed. The tomb was uncovered and Constantine built a church over it.

That church was destroyed by the Persians in 614. Several other churches were rebuilt on this site. The present one is the work of the Crusaders, completed in the twelfth century. It included under one closed compound both the tomb and the rock of Golgotha, where Jesus was crucified.

In the center of the rotunda of the church is a small chamber, the Chapel of the Angel. A narrow passageway leads from it to the Holy Sepulchre. A marble plaque marks where Jesus was buried.

In the upper portion of the church, about fifteen feet above the floor, is the rock of Golgotha.

Also inside the church is the Chapel of St. Helena. In the crypt beneath it, the Empress Helena, mother of Constantine the Great, was reputed to have found the True Cross in 325.

**Bethlehem** — *View of Bethlehem from the bell tower of the Church of the Nativity.*

# BETHLEHEM

*"And it came to pass, as the angels were gone away from them into heaven, the shepherds said one to another, Let us now go even unto Bethlehem ... And they came with haste, and found Mary, and Joseph, and the babe lying in a manger."* LUKE 2:15, 16.

Bethlehem is an ancient village that has been in existence since the time of Jacob. It stands on top of a rocky hill, some 2,500 feet high, about five miles north of Jerusalem. Here Ruth gleaned behind the reapers in the fields of Boaz. It is David's birthplace, and in the fields, below, the angels announced to the shepherds that the Savior was born.

Many caves or grottos are found on the hillside, and from early times one of these was identified as the cave of the manger, where Jesus was born. In 326, the Roman Emperor Constantine, a convert to Christianity, built the first Church of the Nativity over the manger and grotto of the Nativity. In the sixth century, the Byzantine Emperor Justinian rebuilt and enlarged the church as it stands today.

When the Persians invaded the Holy Land in 614, they destroyed many churches in nearby Jerusalem, but they spared the church in Bethlehem. They saw that the Magi as depicted in a mosaic inside the church resembled their own ancestors and out of respect for them left this shrine untouched.

On Christmas, 1100, the Crusader, Baldwin I, Count of Flanders, was crowned King of the Latin Kingdom of Jerusalem here and ordered high walls and towers built around the church to protect it.

Today, the Church of Nativity is the oldest church in the world still in use. Inside, narrow steps lead down to the Grotto of Nativity. There, on the marble floor beneath the Altar of the Nativity a large silver star was placed in 1717 to mark the place where Jesus was born. Daily masses are held in the Grotto.

**Tomb of Lazarus** — *The traditional site of the tomb from which Jesus raised Lazarus.*

# BETHANY

*"Now a certain man was sick, named Lazarus, of Bethany, the town of Mary and her sister Martha."* JOHN 11:1.

Lazarus was the brother of Mary and Martha, and all were friends of Jesus. When their brother was dying, the sisters went to get Jesus. But He did not approach Bethany until after Lazarus was dead and had been buried several days. When Martha met him, Jesus told her, "I am the resurrection, and the life: he that believeth in me, though he were dead, yet shall he live." (John 11:25) Then Jesus ordered the stone removed from the tomb and called Lazarus to come out. Rising from the dead, clothed in his burial garments, Lazarus came to them.

Jesus returned to Bethany six days before the Last Supper, attending a supper at the house of Simon the leper. Among the guests was Lazarus.

Today, Bethany is a small village of old houses surrounded by ruins on the eastern slope of the Mount of Olives. It is on the road from Jericho to Jerusalem, less than two miles away.

The Tomb of Lazarus is here, its entrance near the new church. Some twenty stone steps down in a narrow passage is a chamber about eight feet square, where Lazarus was buried.

In the fourth century, there was a church near Lazarus' tomb. Part of its mosaic floor may be seen outside the present church in the courtyard to its west. This mosaic is decorated with small crosses. Inside the western part of the church are the remains of the mosaic floor of the second church built in Bethany, some time before the sixth century. No crosses are included in its design because, in 427, the Emperor Theodosius ordered that no cross be placed in a pavement, which could be stepped upon. The present Church of St. Lazarus was dedicated in 1954.

**Jericho** — *The Mount of Temptation where Jesus fasted and was tempted by Satan.*

# JERICHO

*"And it came to pass, that as he was come nigh unto Jericho, a certain blind man sat by the way side begging ... And he cried, saying, Jesus, thou son of David, have mercy upon me."*
LUKE 18:35,38.

Here at Jericho, known as the city of palm trees, Jesus restored sight to Bartimaeus and his companion. Here He also brought salvation to the rich man, Zacchaeus, at whose house he rested. The story in the parable of the Good Samaritan takes place on the road from Jericho to Jerusalem.

Jericho's importance in the Bible goes back to the time of Joshua, when he was leading the Israelites into the Promised Land. The walled Canaanite city of Jericho barred their way. Following divine command, for seven days Joshua and his army marched around this city and on the seventh circuit of the seventh day, as the seven priests blew their trumpets and the army shouted, Jericho's wall tumbled down. After destroying the city and killing most of its inhabitants, Joshua predicted that if anyone tried to rebuild it, he would lose his eldest son when he started the walls, and his youngest son when he set up the gates. Centuries later, Hiel the Bethelite lost his two sons as he fortified Jericho.

Located some seventeen miles east of Jerusalem and lying some eight hundred feet below sea level, Jericho's tropical climate with its lush foliage attracted Herod the Great to build his elaborate winter capital here.

Today, one can see the ruins of Herod's palace, as well as the archeological excavation which puts Jericho's origin back to about 10,000 years ago and makes it one of the oldest, if not the oldest, cities in the world.

Fronted by double pools, the Spring of Elisha waters a large oasis by Jericho. This was the bitter water the prophet Elisha purified by casting salt in it.

West of Jericho the Mount of Temptation, where Jesus fasted for forty days and was tempted by the devil, rises from the plain.

**Hebron —** *Fortress over the Cave of Machpelah where Sarah and Abraham are buried.*

# HEBRON

*"And Sarah died in Kirjatharba; the same is Hebron in the land of Canaan: and Abraham came to mourn for Sarah, and to weep for her."* GENESIS 23:2

When Sarah died at the age of one hundred and twenty-seven years, Abraham bought the Cave of Machpelah at Hebron from Ephron the Hittite for four hundred shekels of silver. Later, Abraham was buried here, as were Isaac, and Jacob, Rebecca and Leah. According to one Jewish tradition, Adam and Eve lived near here after their expulsion from the Garden of Eden and were also buried in the cave. Herod the Great built a fortress-like structure around the Cave of Machpelah. After its capture by Joshua, it became the capital of the tribe of Judah.

For over seven years before he captured Jerusalem, David made Hebron his capital. Abner, the commander of Saul's army, was murdered and buried here. Ish-Bosheth, one of Saul's sons, who fought against David and was beheaded, had his head buried in the grave of his former friend, Abner.

Absalom, David's son, was born here and it was in Hebron that Absalom started his unsuccessful rebellion against his father.

One of the oldest still inhabited cities of the world, Hebron is about twenty miles south of Jerusalem and three thousand feet up in the hills. It is a colorful, old city with stone houses and narrow winding streets. Until recently, it was almost exclusively inhabited by Arabs.

A mosque, originally a Byzantine church and later a Crusader's church, is built above the cave that holds the tombs of the patriarchs. Stone cenotaphs mark the place of their burial below.

**Beersheba—***An oasis in the semi-desert area around the ancient city.*

# BEERSHEBA

*"Thus they made a covenant at Beersheba: then Abimelech rose up, and Phicol the chief captain of his host, and they returned into the land of the Philistines."* GENESIS 21:32

Abraham built a well at Beersheba and there he and Abimelech, the king of Gerar, agreed to keep peace between them. To show his goodwill and as a token of the covenant they had made, Abraham gave Abimelech seven ewe lambs. The name Beersheba means "well of seven."

From that well, Abraham left with his son Isaac, who God had ordered Abraham to sacrifice on Mount Moriah, and Jacob left on his journey to Haran in Mesopotamia.

Beersheba is some thirty-six miles southwest of Hebron in a semi-desert area. It was considered the southern end of the Holy Land, and the saying, "From Dan even to Beersheba," became proverbial (Judges 20:1).

The sons of Samuel served here as judges and Elijah passed through the town on his way to Horeb.

About two thousand years before Abraham's time, as far back as 4000 B.C., Beersheba had been settled by a people who dug their houses twenty feet under the hot ground. On the land above their subterranean homes, they grew wheat and barley. Excavations of this ancient underground village may be seen at Abu Matar, a few miles from modern Beersheba.

The present city was founded after Israel's independence. In 1947, the town was almost abandoned and consisted of only a few narrow streets.

Today, nearly 100,000 people live here and modern apartment houses tower over the old stone homes. At the end of Keren Kaymet Street is an ancient well dating back to the time of Abraham and bearing his name.

On Thursday, the Bedouins who live nearby come into town to hold an open air market, where they sell everything from camel meat to Arabian handicrafts.

**Joppa (Jaffa)** — *The ancient port from which Jonah sailed.*

# JOPPA (JAFFA)

*"But Peter put them all forth, and kneeled down, and prayed; and turning him to the body said, Tabitha, arise. And she opened her eyes: and when she saw Peter, she sat up."* ACTS 9:40.

Peter lived in Joppa in the house of Simon the tanner until the servants of Cornelius invited him to Caeserea. He was brought to the death chamber of a charitable Christian woman, Tabitha, who lived in the port city of Joppa. After praying by her body, Peter brought her back to life.

The city was named after Noah's son, Japheth. It is one of the oldest ports in the world, serving Jerusalem some thirty-five miles away. The cedars used in Solomon's temple were floated from Lebanon down the Mediterranean coast to Joppa and from there carried overland to Jerusalem.

It was from Joppa that Jonah started his voyage during which he was swallowed by a great fish.

During the Crusades, the vital port changed hands several times. In 1799, Napoleon conquered it, destroying much of the city.

Today, Joppa is an Arab city in Israel and it is a picturesque confusion of old houses and alley ways. Joppa is being turned into an art and entertainment center. Several mosques may be visited in the city including a little mosque in an alley near the Monastery of St. Peter, which reputedly is on the site of the home of Simon the tanner.

Right next to this old port city is Joppa's modern sister city, Tel Aviv. Until its founding in 1909, only sand dunes were to be seen where Tel Aviv now rises.

**Samaritans** — *Present-day Samaritans in the city where the Samaritan woman gave Jesus water.*

# SHECHEM

*"And Jacob came to Shalem, a city of Shechem, which is in the land of Canaan, when he went from Padanaram; and pitched his tent before the city."* GENESIS 33:18.

Before Jacob came to Shechem, Abraham had camped near that city and found it occupied by Canaanites, despite God's promise that it would belong to his descendants.

When Jacob came here, he bought some land for a hundred pieces of silver from the Hivites. On that land, Joseph's brothers grazed their flocks. When Joseph died in Egypt, his mummified body was brought back to Shechem for burial.

Shechem was one of the six "cities of refuge" of the Old Testament. In such a city, anyone who had committed an accidental killing could escape all avengers. He would be tried and if found guilty of deliberate murder, he would be executed. But if he had not killed willfully, he could live safely in a city of refuge. When the high priest died, the matter was considered ended and he could return home, safe from avengers.

Joshua assembled the twelve tribes at Shechem to hear his farewell words and to pledge them to worship the God of Israel.

Later, it became the headquarters of the Samaritans and a few hundred still live nearby. On the adjacent Mount Gerizim, which rises 2,890 feet, is a Samaritan shrine. During Passover, the Samaritans make a sacrifice on the mountain and camp there.

About a mile from the present city are the ruins of ancient Shechem at Tell Balatah. Nearby is Jacob's Well, where Jesus asked the Samaritan woman for a drink of water. A Greek Orthodox Church houses the still usable well.

A short distance northwest of Jacob's Well a domed Moslem building rises over a stone grave, where Joseph is believed to be buried.

**Caesarea** – *Part of the sea mole built by Herod the Great, at the Roman port capital of Palestine.*

# CAESAREA

*"And the morrow after they entered into Caeserea. And Cornelius waited for them, and had called together his kinsmen and near friends. And as Peter was coming in, Cornelius met him, and fell down at this feet, and worshipped him. But Peter took him up, saying, Stand up; I myself also am a man."*
ACTS 10:24-26

When Peter baptized the Roman centurion Cornelius, he converted the first non-Jew, thus beginning the conversion of the Gentiles. This important event occurred in Caeserea.

Later, when Peter was escaping possible death in Jerusalem, he came to this port and sailed for Tarsus, his home in Asia Minor. Peter returned to Caeserea twice and finally was brought here as a prisoner. As Caeserea served as the Roman capital of Palestine, Peter was put on trial here before Festus and Agrippa.

Philip the Evangelist lived and preached here.

At the time of Jesus, Caeserea was an important port on the Mediterranean, which had been rebuilt by Herod the Great between 28-14 B.C. Herod had a sea mole constructed which was two hundred feet wide and which stood in a hundred and twenty feet of water. To build this huge sea wall, fifty-foot-long cut stone blocks each weighing over twenty tons had to be lowered into place. The completed port was as large as the one serving Athens and was one of the most famous ports of its time. Herod also built a theater and a hippodrome seating 20,000.

In A.D. 66, the Jewish revolt against the Romans started here and ended with the fall of Masada in A.D. 73.

During the Crusades this vital port changed hands several times. After Baldwin I, the first Crusader king of Jerusalem captured Caeserea, legend relates that he found, but then lost the Holy Grail, the cup which Jesus used at the Last Supper.

**Mount Tabor** — *The church built on the traditional site of Jesus' Transfiguration.*

# MOUNT TABOR

*"And after six days Jesus taketh Peter, James, and John his brother, and bringeth them up into an high mountain apart, And was tranfigured before them: and his face did shine as the sun, and his raiment was white as the light."* MATTHEW 17:1-2.

Traditionally, Mount Tabor is where Jesus took His three disciples and they witnessed His Transfiguration. They saw Moses and Elijah talking to Jesus. They heard the voice saying "this is my beloved Son."It was after His Transfiguration that Jesus knew of the suffering that would mark the way to His coming glory.

In the Old Testament, Mount Tabor is near the place where the Jewish prophetess Deborah rallied her people to fight under Barak against the Canaanite charioteers led by Sisera. The Canaanites were defeated and, in their flight, most of them drowned in the nearby Kishon River.

In 1799, history repeated itself, as Napoleon defeated the Arabs and Turks close to Mount Tabor and, in their flight, many drowned in the same river.

Rising 1,843 feet high above sea level and some twelve miles southwest of the lower end of the Sea of Galilee, Mount Tabor is steep-sided and somewhat cone-shaped with a partly flattened top. From here, one has a breath-taking view of snow-capped Mount Hermon far to the north, while to the south lies Mount Gilboa, where King Saul and his son Jonathan were slain by the Philistines.

**The River Jordan** – *The river in which John the Baptist baptized Jesus.*

# BETHABARA

*"Then cometh Jesus from Galilee to Jordan unto John, to be baptized of him ... And Jesus, when he was baptized, went up straightway out of the water: and, lo, the heavens were opened unto him, and he saw the Spirit of God descending like a dove and lighting upon him: And lo a voice from heaven, saying, This is my beloved Son, in whom I am well pleased."* MATTHEW 3:13,16,17.

Bethabara is believed to be the site of where John baptized Jesus (John 1:28). It is located on the Jordan River five miles north of the Dead Sea and six miles east of Jericho.

The name Bethabara means, "house at the ford." It would be a natural place for people to gather to hear the words of John who proclaimed that he was preparing the way for "one mightier than myself". John selected the site on the river as a suitable one for "A baptism of repentence for the remission of sins".

The waters of the Jordan River start from the springs of Mount Heron in Syria, and the river winds about two hundred miles through the Holy Land before emptying into the Dead Sea, whose surface is 1,286 feet below sea level.

As early as A.D. 333, Bethabara is mentioned as a stopping place for pilgrims to the Holy Land. In the sixth century, the site of Jesus' baptism was marked here by a marble column topped with an iron cross.

Today, several churches are located around this historic place. On Epiphany Sunday, a special service of blessing the water is held at the Greek Monastery of St. John.

Across from Bethabara is a small hill known as the Mount of St. Elijah. This is reputedly where "a chariot of fire and horses of fire" took Elijah from his disciple Elisha and "Elijah went up by a whirlwind into heaven."

**Nazareth –** *Church of the Annunciation where the angel Gabriel appeared to Mary.*

# NAZARETH

*"And in the sixth month the angel Gabriel was sent from God unto a city of Galilee, named Nazareth, To a virgin espoused to a man whose name was Joseph, of the house of David; and the virgin's name was Mary. And the angel came in unto her, and said, Hail, thou that art highly favoured, the Lord is with thee: blessed art thou among women ... And, behold, thou shalt conceive in thy womb, and bring forth a son, and shalt call his name Jesus."* LUKE 1:26-28,31.

Nazareth is the revered scene of the Annunciation where the angel Gabriel told Mary that she would give birth to Jesus. Here Jesus lived during most of His first thirty years. In the small village's synagogue, Jesus studied and later preached. The suggestion that He was the Messiah angered Jesus' fellow townsmen and they threatened to hurl Him from a precipice. The precipice from which Jesus was nearly hurled may have been near the Maronite church. After this, Jesus is not known to have returned to Nazareth.

Descendants of His family did remain in Nazareth into at least the second century, when the two grandsons of Jude, the brother of Jesus, are known to have lived here.

Still in use is Mary's Well, where Mary drew water for her family.

The site of Jesus' home is claimed by both the Churches of St. Joseph and St. Gabriel.

The Church of St. Joseph is built on the site of his workshop and is near the Church of the Annunciation.

Nazareth's most important shrine is the Church of the Annunciation. It was built over the ruins of several earlier churches including one erected by the Crusaders, who made this town one of the goals of their Crusade. Below the main level of the church is the grotto, where Mary was visited by the angel, and contains the "Column of Gabriel".

**Sea of Galilee —** *The old city of Tiberias on the shore of the sea Jesus calmed.*

# THE SEA OF GALILEE

*"But the ship was now in the midst of the sea, tossed with waves: for the wind was contrary. And in the fourth watch of the night Jesus went unto them, walking on the sea."*
MATTHEW 14:24-25.

The waters Jesus walked on were those of the Sea of Galilee and here He calmed the wind.

In Jesus' time some two million Jews lived in the Holy Land and most of them lived around the Sea of Galilee. Many of the places mentioned in the New Testament are along the shores of Galilee: Capernaum; Bethsaida; Cana; Magdala, where Mary Magdalene was born; Chorazin, whose destruction Jesus predicted and whose ruins may still be seen today.

Despite its name, the Sea of Galilee is a body of fresh water, fed by the Jordan River. It measures 12¾ miles from the northern entrance to the southern exit of the Jordan and is 7¼ miles at its widest point. The Sea of Galilee is about seven hundred feet below the level of the Mediterranean. Low hills encircle most of the lake, although some rise to above 3,000 feet. Just as in the time of Jesus, Galilee is filled with fish. Olives, figs and pomegranates grow along the nearby valleys and slopes.

Today, the most important city on the lake is Tiberias. Built about A.D. 20 by Herod Antipas, the son of Herod the Great, Tiberias was probably not visited by Jesus. After the second destruction of the Temple, Tiberias became an important center of Jewish learning. Several Jewish religious leaders were buried here, including Maimonides, the twelfth century physician and philosopher. The fortresses, whose ruins are found around Tiberias and the lake, are the work of the Crusaders, who built them in the twelfth century.

Because it is below sea level, Galilee has a semi-tropical climate and when cold air flows down from snow-topped Mount Hermon, storms still sweep across the waters Jesus calmed.

**Cana** — *The place where Jesus turned water into wine.*

# CANA

*Jesus saith unto them, Fill the waterpots with water. And they filled them to the brim. And he saith unto them, Draw out now, and bear unto the governor of the feast. And they bare it. When the ruler of the feast had tasted the water that was made wine, and knew not whence it was . . . the governor of the feast called the bridegroom, And saith . . . thou hast kept the good wine until now.* JOHN 2:7-9, 10

Cana was the village where Jesus performed His first two miracles. While attending a marriage feast, Jesus turned the water into wine. It was here also that a nobleman came to Jesus telling Him that his son was dying in nearby Capernaum. Jesus assured the nobleman that his son would live. The man believing in Christ's words, started home to see his son. On the way, his servants met him and told him that his son was alive, and that he had begun to recover at the very moment the nobleman talked to Jesus.

The name Cana means, "place of the reeds" and it is near the Sea of Galilee, several miles northeast of Nazareth. It was the home of the disciple Nathanael.

Today, several churches mark the reputed site of ancient Cana. The Latin church is on the ruins of an old basilica that dates back to the time of Emperor Constantine in the fourth century and has a partially preserved mosaic floor. In one of the churches are urns that some believe to be those used by Jesus when He turned the water into wine.

**Capernaum** — *The synagogue where Jesus prophesied the fall of "his own city."*

# CAPERNAUM

*"And when Jesus was entered into Capernaum, there came unto him a centurion, beseeching him, And saying, Lord, my servant lieth at home sick of the palsy, grievously tormented. And Jesus saith unto him, I will come and heal him."*
MATTHEW 8:5-7.

On the northwest shore of the Sea of Galilee, a few miles from where the Jordan River enters the great lake, lies Capernaum. This was the second home of Jesus and was known as "his own city." Here, He preached and performed many miracles.

Jesus lived in this Roman garrison town after leaving Nazareth. Capernaum was the scene of many of the miracles of Jesus. Here He healed the centurion's servant of palsy, and Peter's mother-in-law of fever, and it was here that He brought Jairus' daughter back to life.

It was at Capernaum that Jesus saw Matthew "sitting at the receipt of custom" and called him as an apostle.

Jesus preached in the synagogue which had previously been built by the centurion, whose servant He had cured. But despite His teaching, the people found no need to repent, nor change their ways. Jesus predicted that the town would be reduced to ruins.

During the Jewish-Roman wars near the end of the first century, the synagogue was destroyed. It was rebuilt in the third century, but then fell to ruins again.

Today, a Franciscan monastery stands near the partly restored synagogue. In 1894, the Franciscans acquired the site, but fearing the unsettled conditions, they covered over the ruins and planted above them so no Arab would take any of the ancient stones. In the early 1900s, they began excavating and restoring the synagogue. While the building is Roman in style, it shows the Jewish influence especially in the orientation in the direction of Jerusalem, and in the upper gallery, where the women sat separately from the men.

**The Loaves and Fishes** — *Mosaic in the Church of the Multiplication in Bethsaida.*

# BETHSAIDA

*"And he commanded the multitude to sit down on the grass, and took the five loaves, and the two fishes, and looking up to heaven, he blessed, and brake, and gave the loaves to his disciples, and the disciples to the multitude. And they did all eat, and were filled ... And they that had eaten were about five thousand men, beside women and children."* MATTHEW 14:19-21

It was to this town by the Sea of Galilee that Jesus went after learning of the murder of John the Baptist.

Finding Himself followed by a multitude, Jesus had them sit down on a large field by Bethsaida. Miraculously, He fed all five thousand people from just five loaves and two small fish.

Bethsaida may roughly be translated as, "place of fishing" an appropriate name for a village by the lake's western shore. It was the home of Peter, Andrew and Philip, who left their fishing nets to follow Jesus.

In the fourth century, the stone upon which Jesus put the bread to feed the five thousand was being used an altar. Pilgrims took away chips from it, believing its chips would hold healing powers.

Near the springs of Tabgha, as it is now known, in a Byzantine church called the Church of the Multiplication, which dates from the 4th century, is a mosaic floor which depicts the story of the loaves and fishes.

In the nearby chapel is the rock called "Mensa Domini" (The Table of The Lord) upon which it is believed that Jesus ate with the Apostles after naming Peter foremost among them.

Also rising nearby is a hill that tradition claims to be the Mount of the Beatitudes, where Jesus delivered the Sermon on the Mount. From its church, there is a charming view over Galilee.

# TRAVEL INFORMATION

CURRENCY: The basic unit of currency is the Israeli pound, which is divided into 100 agorots. As the value of the American dollar compared to the Israeli pound may change, check upon your arrival to learn the current rate of exchange. Travelers checks and credit cards are widely accepted.

LANGUAGE: Hebrew and Arabic are the official languages. But English is commonly spoken, especially at major hotels and tourist sites.

WHAT TO BUY: Yemenite embroidered blouses and other clothes are attractive. The contemporary ceremics are handsome. Shoes and leather goods may be a good buy. Silver and gold filagree jewelry can be found in the flea market of Joppa, where it is sold by weight. Be careful about buying "antique" pottery, statues and coins.

SPECIAL TIPS: The Jewish Sabbath begins at sunset on Friday and ends at sunset on Saturday. In some hotel dining rooms, you may see a sign requesting you not to smoke during the Sabbath. If there is an ashtray on your table, feel free to smoke.

The electric current in the Holy Land is 220 volts so do not use 110 volt electric shavers, curlers, etc. without a conversion plug. Buy the plug before leaving.

Film is more expensive in the Holy Land than in the United States and you are legally allowed to bring in up to ten rolls of film or ten reels of movie film.

Medical and dental care are easily available, of high standards and at modest fees.

DOCUMENTS: Citizens of the United States need only a valid passport to enter the Holy Land (Israel). If you do not have a passport, inquire at your local post office how to obtain one. You should check with your travel agent or airline to learn if any health documents will be required for your trip.

HOW TO GO THERE: Several major airlines fly there and at certain times of the year, it is possible to go by ship.

ACCOMMODATIONS: These range from Christian hospices to a guest house in a collective settlement or kibbutz or to luxury hotels belonging to international American hotel chains. March to September is the high season, meaning that prices at hotels will be higher then than from October through February.

TOURING: Tours can be arranged before you depart on your trip or they may be arranged once you are in the Holy Land. Numerous sight-seeing buses with English-speaking guides go to all the important sites. Rental, self-drive cars can be obtained and the roads are good and well marked. One unique feature of traveling within cities or even from city to city is the "sherut" taxi, which you share with other passengers, thus reducing your own fare. Using a major city such as Jerusalem or Haifa as a base, you can make day tours to most of the sites in the south or north without constantly changing hotels and repacking.

CLOTHES: The dress is mostly informal, ties rarely being required. Lightweight clothing is best between March and October. Women should dress conservatively when touring religious shrines or visiting Orthodox Jewish sections. Comfortable walking shoes are a must. Because of the brilliant light, sunglasses are helpful. If you enjoy swimming be sure to take a bathingsuit for you can swim in the Mediterranean, the Red Sea, the Sea of Galilee or "sit" on the salty, bouyant waters of the Dead Sea.